HAL•LEONARD UKULELE PLAY-ALONG

GREEN DAY

CONTENTS

Ukulele by Chris Kringel
Tracking, mixing, and mastering by Jake Johnson and Chris Kringel
Cover Photo © Bob Gruen / www.bobgruen.com

ISBN 978-1-4768-7557-6

HAL•LEONARD® CORPORATION
7777 W. BLUEMOUND RD. P.O. BOX 13819 MILWAUKEE, WI 53213

In Australia Contact:
Hal Leonard Australia Pty. Ltd.
4 Lentara Court
Cheltenham, Victoria, 3192 Australia
Email: ausadmin@halleonard.com.au

Visit Hal Leonard Online at
www.halleonard.com

Basket Case

Words by Billie Joe
Music by Green Day

© 1994 WB MUSIC CORP. and GREEN DAZE MUSIC
All Rights Administered by WB MUSIC CORP.
All Rights Reserved   Used by Permission

2

me.   It all keeps add - ing up. _

_   I think I'm crack - ing up. _____   Am

I just par - a - noid? ___   Am I just stoned? _

3. I

Verse

went to a shrink ___   to an - a - lyze my dreams. _
went to a whore, __   who said my life's a bore. ___

___   She says it's lack of sex ___
___   So quit my whin - ing 'cause _

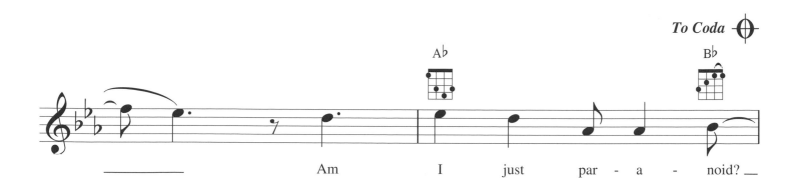

Am I just par - a - noid?

Interlude

Yeah, yeah, yeah.

*Sung 1st time only.

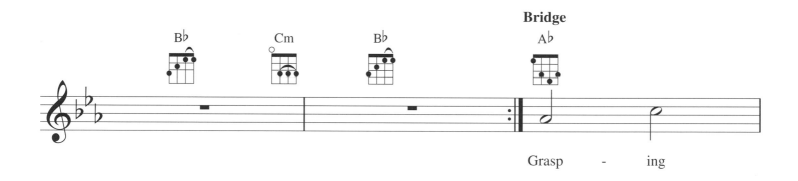

Bridge

Grasp - ing

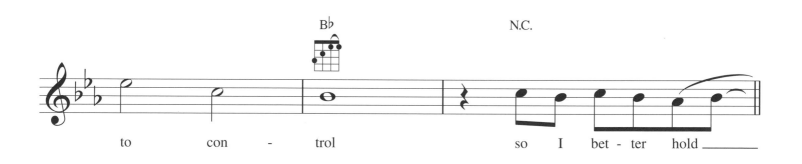

to con - trol

so I bet - ter hold

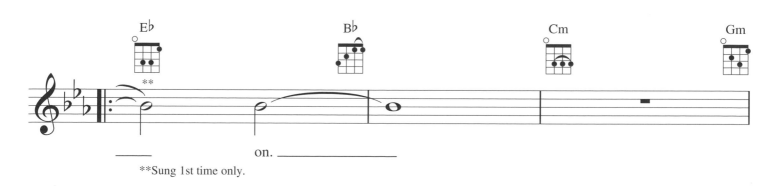

on.

**Sung 1st time only.

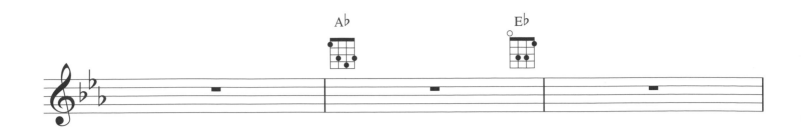

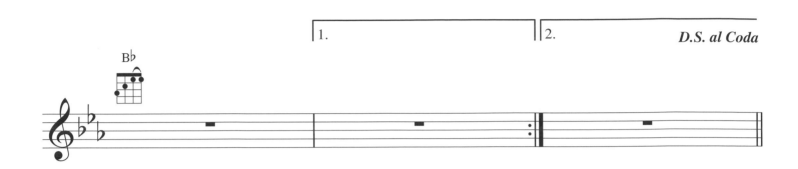

Am   I   just   stoned? ____

*Sung 1st time only.

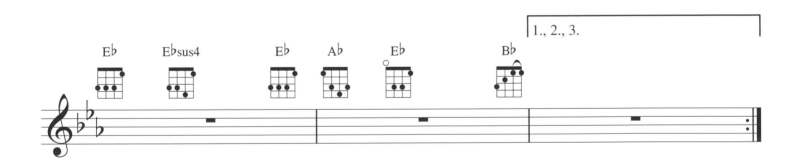

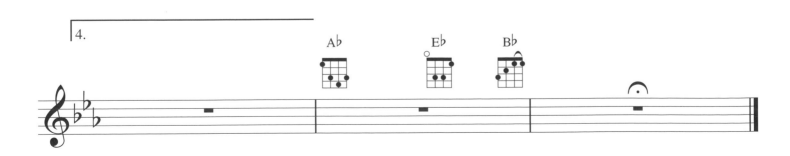

TRACK 5

Good Riddance
(Time of Your Life)

Words by Billie Joe
Music by Green Day

First note

Intro
Moderately slow, in 2 ♩ = 96

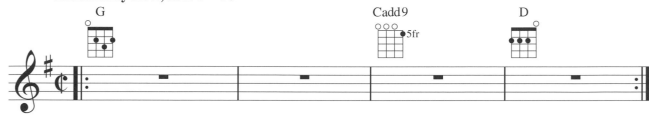

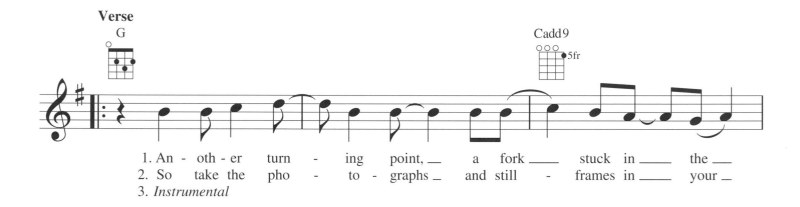

1. An - oth - er turn - ing point, ___ a fork ___ stuck in ___ the ___
2. So take the pho - to - graphs ___ and still - frames in ___ your ___
3. *Instrumental*

road.   Time grabs you by ___ the ___ wrist, ___ di - rects ___
mind.   Hang it on ___ a ___ shelf ___ in good ___

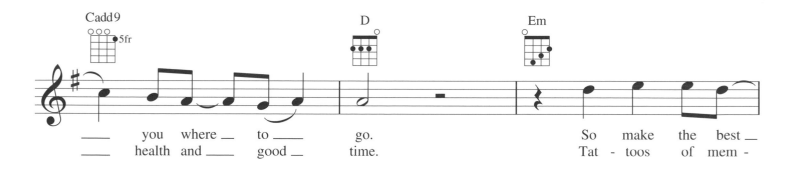

___ you where ___ to ___ go.   So make the best ___
___ health and ___ good ___ time.   Tat - toos of mem -

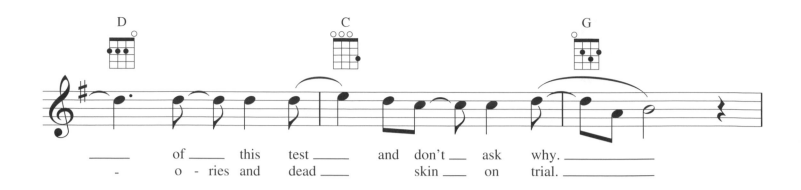

_____ of _____ this test _____ and don't _____ ask why. _____
- o - ries and dead _____ skin _____ on trial. _____

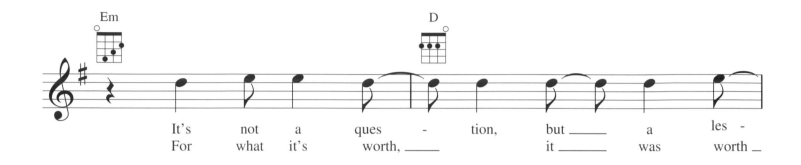

It's   not   a   ques - tion,   but _____   a   les -
For   what   it's   worth, _____   it _____   was   worth _____

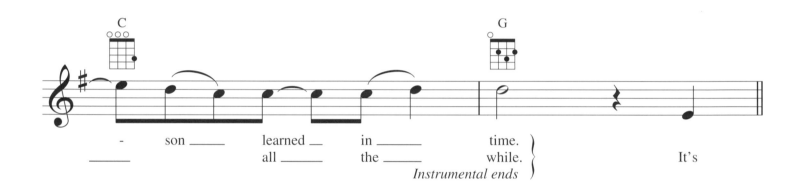

- son _____ learned _____ in _____ time.
_____ all _____ the _____ while.   *Instrumental ends*   It's

𝄋 Chorus

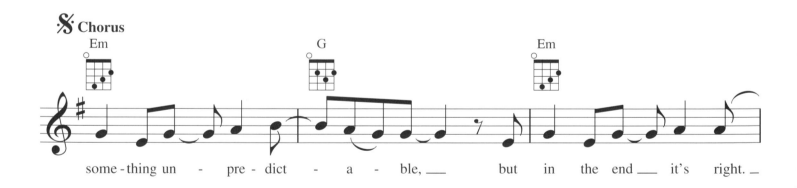

some - thing un - pre - dict - a - ble, _____ but in the end _____ it's right. _____

To Coda ⊕

_____ I   hope   you   had _____   the   time _____   of _____   your   life. _____

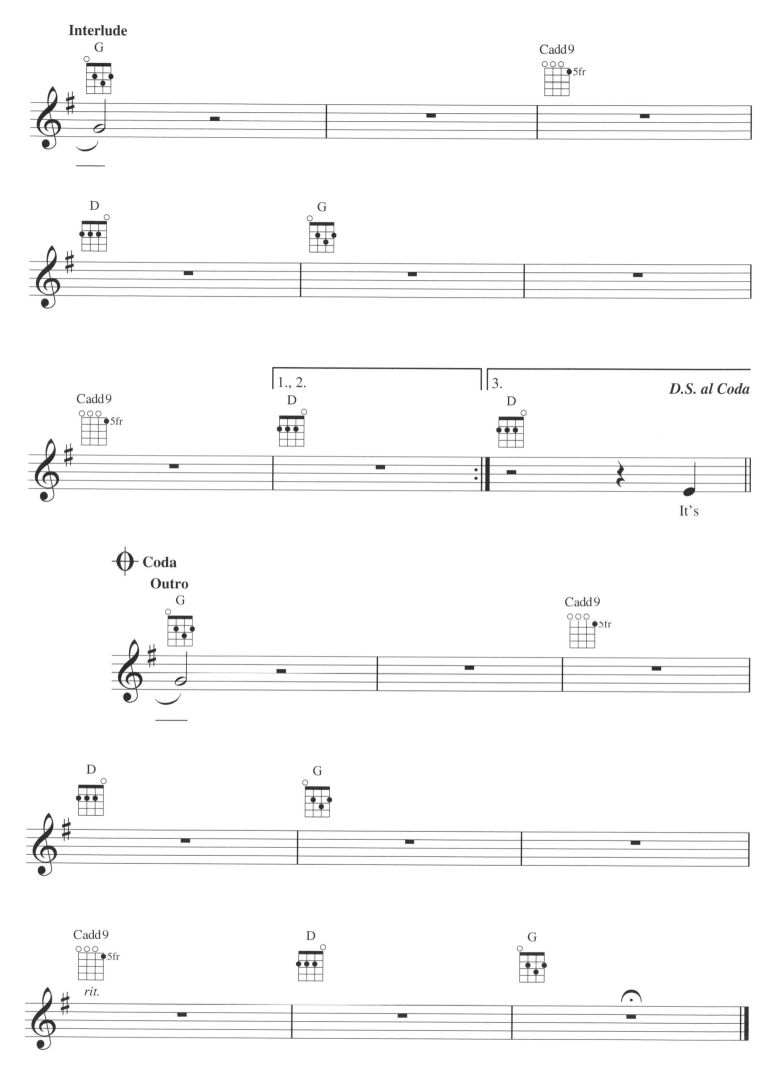

It's

TRACK 3

Boulevard of Broken Dreams

Words by Billie Joe
Music by Green Day

First note

Intro
Moderately slow ♩ = 84

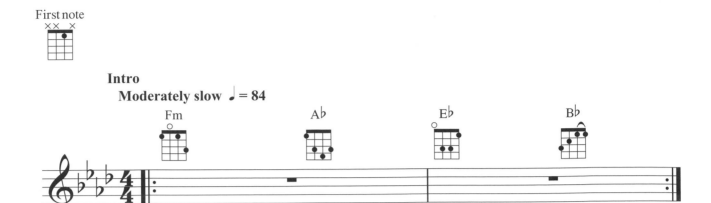

Verse

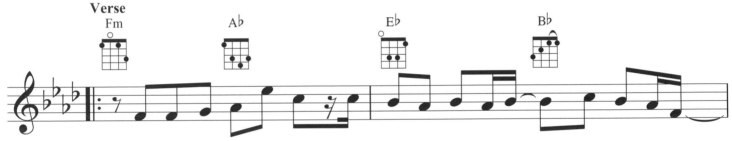

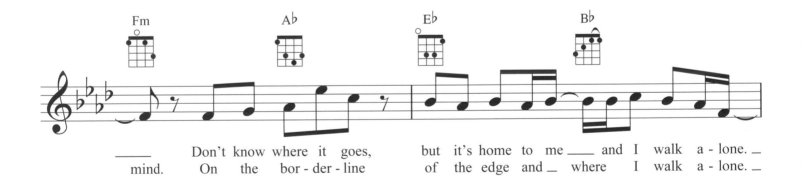

1. I walk a lone-ly road, the on-ly one that I _____ have ev-er known. _
2. I'm walk-ing down the line that di-vides me _ some-where in my _

_____ Don't know where it goes, but it's home to me _____ and I walk a-lone. _
mind. On the bor-der-line of the edge and _ where I walk a-lone. _

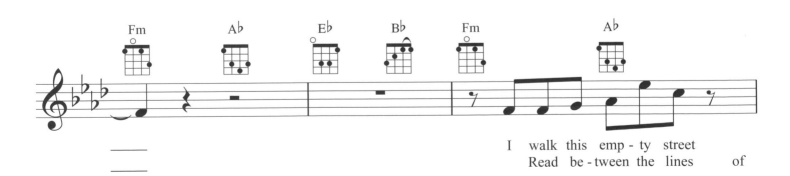

_____
_____ I walk this emp-ty street
Read be-tween the lines of

on the bou - le - vard ___ of bro - ken dreams, _ where the cit - y sleeps and
what's fucked up and ___ ev - ery thing's al - right. Check my vi - tal signs and

I'm the on - ly one ___ and I walk a - lone. ___)
know I'm still a - live ___ and I walk a - lone. ___)

I walk a - lone, ___ I walk a - lone. ___

Chorus

I walk a - lone, ___ I walk a... My shad - ow's the on -

- ly one that walks ___ be - side _ me. My shal - low heart's _

___ the on - ly thing ___ that's beat - ing. Some - times ___ I wish _

some - one out there ___ will find ___ me. 'Til then ___ I walk ___

___ a - lone. ___   Ah. ___   Ah. ___   Ah. ___   Ah. ___

1.

2.

___ Ah. ___   Ah. ___   Ah. ___   I walk a - lone, ___ I walk ___ a...

Guitar Solo

1.

2.

Verse

3. I walk this emp - ty street   on the bou - le - vard ___ of bro - ken dreams, ___

12

where the cit - y sleeps and I'm the on - ly one ___ and I walk a...

Chorus

My shad - ow's the on - ly one that walks ___ be - side ___ me.

My shal - low heart's ___ the on - ly thing ___ that's beat - ing.

Some - times ___ I wish ___ some - one out there ___ will find ___ me.

'Til then ___ I walk ___ a - lone. ___

Outro

Holiday

Words by Billie Joe
Music by Green Day

TRACK 7

First note

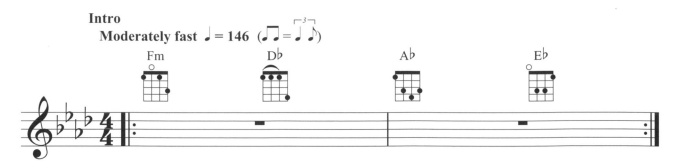

Intro
Moderately fast ♩ = 146

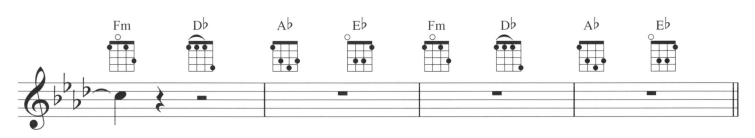

Say,   hey,   cha. _

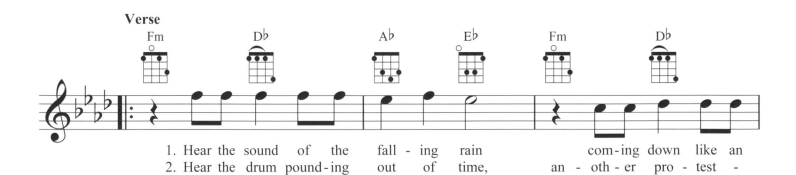

Verse

1. Hear the sound of the fall - ing rain   com - ing down like an
2. Hear the drum pound - ing out of time,   an - oth - er pro - test -

Ar - ma - ged - don flame. The shame,   the ones who died with
or has crossed the line to find the mon - ey's on the

out a name. _____ Hear the dogs howl-ing
oth - er side. _____ Can I get an -

out of key   to a hymn called "Faith and Mis - ery," __
oth - er "A - men?"   There's a flag wrapped a - round a score of

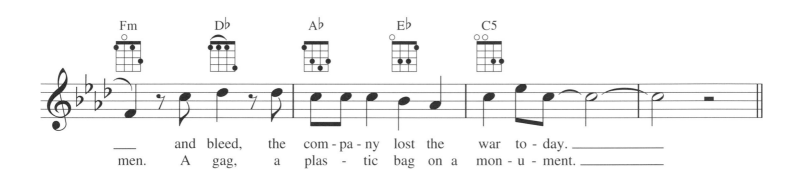

___ and bleed, the com - pa - ny lost the war to - day. _____
men. A gag, a plas - tic bag on a mon - u - ment. _____

Chorus

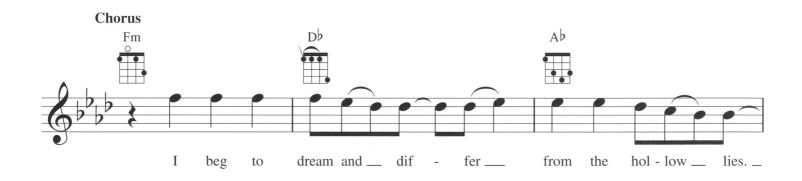

I beg to dream and __ dif - fer __ from the hol - low __ lies. __

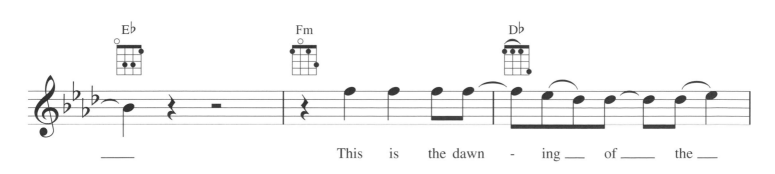

____   This is the dawn - ing __ of ____ the ___

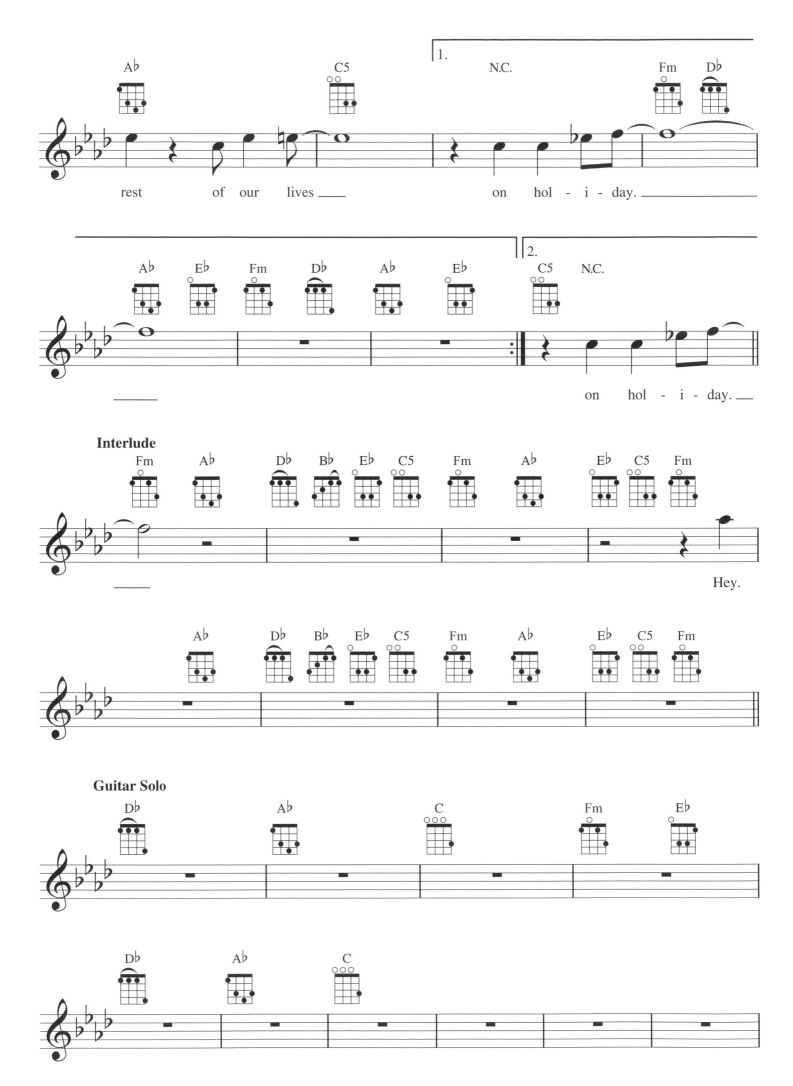

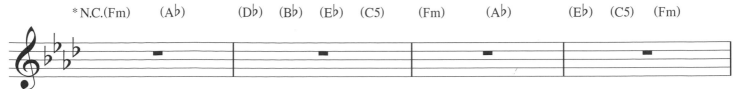

*Chords implied by bass guitar, next 8 measures.

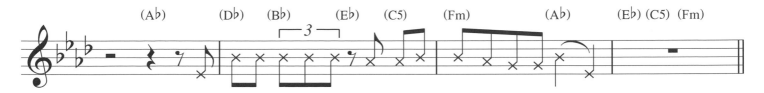

*Spoken: The rep-re-sen-ta-tive from Cal-i - for-nia has the floor. _

Bridge

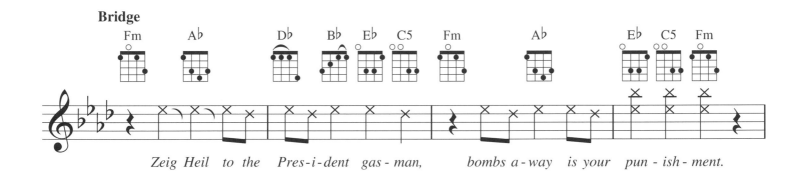

Zeig Heil to the Pres-i-dent gas-man, bombs a-way is your pun-ish-ment.

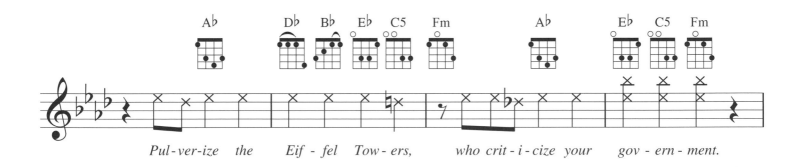

Pul-ver-ize the Eif-fel Tow-ers, who crit-i-cize your gov-ern-ment.

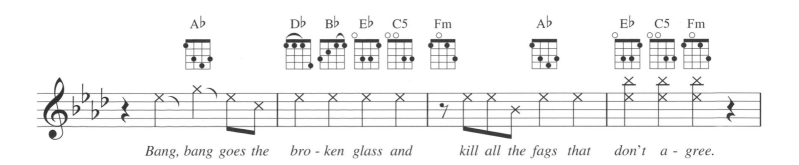

Bang, bang goes the bro-ken glass and kill all the fags that don't a-gree.

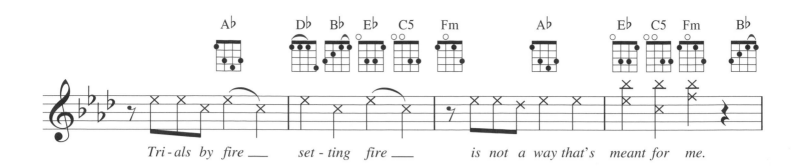

Tri - als by fire ___ set - ting fire ___ is not a way that's meant for me.

Just 'cause   just 'cause, be - cause we're out - laws, yeah.
(Hey, hey,   hey,   hey,   hey,   hey,   hey,   hey.)

Chorus

I beg to dream and ___ dif - fer ___ from the hol - low ___ lies. ___

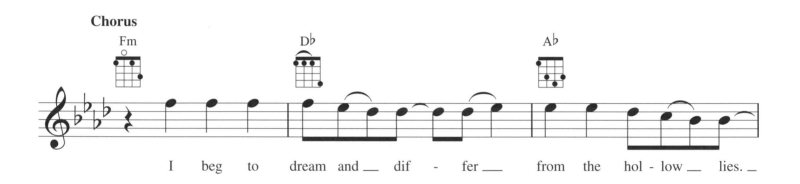

___ This is the dawn - ing ___ of ___ the ___

rest   of our lives. ___   I beg to

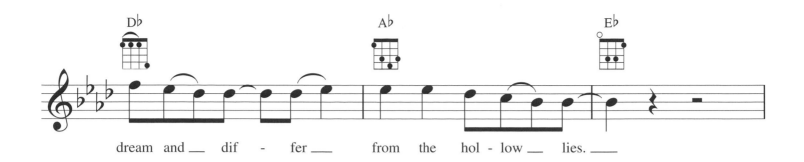

dream and __ dif - fer __ from the hol - low __ lies. __

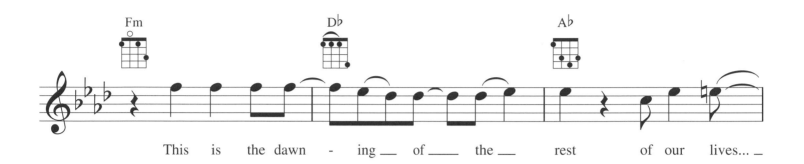

This is the dawn - ing __ of __ the __ rest of our lives... __

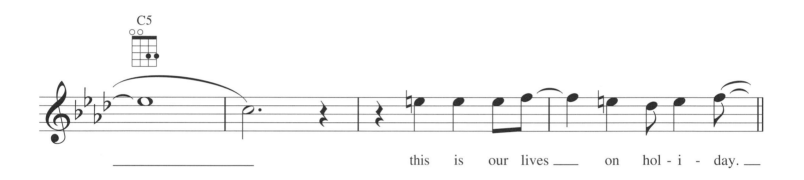

_____ this is our lives __ on hol - i - day. __

Outro

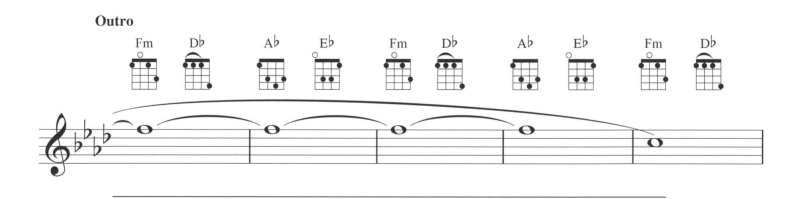

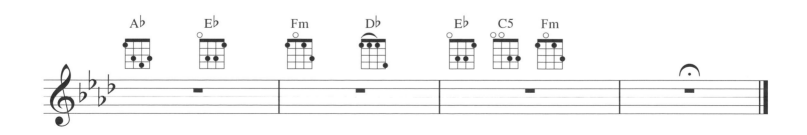

Longview

Words by Billie Joe
Music by Green Day

TRACK 9

First note
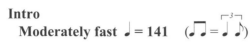

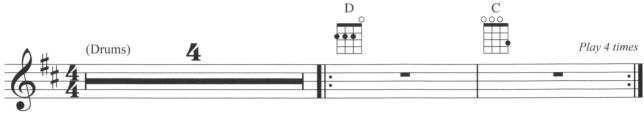

Intro
Moderately fast ♩ = 141

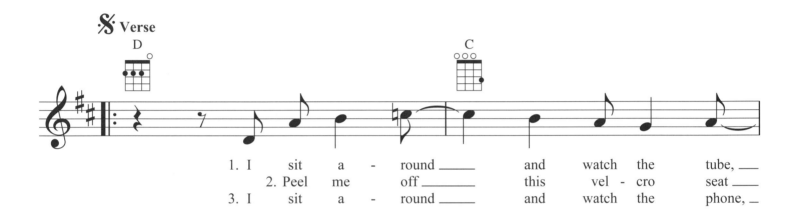

1. I sit a - round _____ and watch the tube, _____
2. Peel me off _____ this vel - cro seat _____
3. I sit a - round _____ and watch the phone, _____

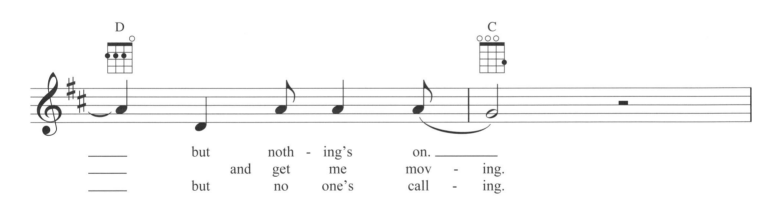

_____ but noth - ing's on. _____
_____ and get me mov - ing.
_____ but no one's call - ing.

I change the chan - nels for an hour _____
I sure as hell _____ can't do it by _____
Call me pa - thet - ic, call me what _____

_____ or two. _____
_____ my - self. _____
_____ you will. _____

Twid - dle my thumbs just for a bit, _____ I'm sick of all _____
I'm feel - ing like a dog in heat, _____ barred in -
My moth - er says to get a job, _____ but she don't like _____

_____ the same old shit. _____ In a house _____
doors from the sum - mer street. _____ I locked the door _____
_____ the one she's got. _____ When mas - tur -

To Coda ⊕

_____ with un - locked doors _____ and I'm fuck - ing la - zy.
_____ to my own cell _____ and I lost the key. _____
ba - tion's lost its fun, _____ you're fuck - ing lone - ly.

Chorus

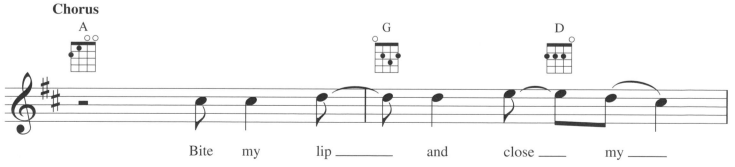

Bite my lip _____ and close _____ my _____

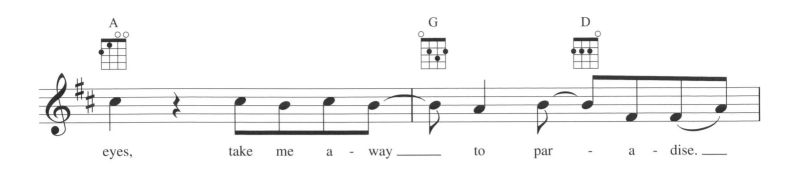

eyes,   take me a - way _____ to par - a - dise. _____

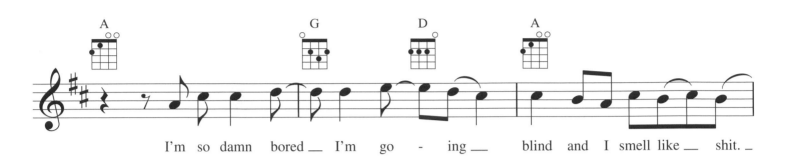

I'm so damn bored _____ I'm go - ing _____ blind and I smell like _____ shit. _____

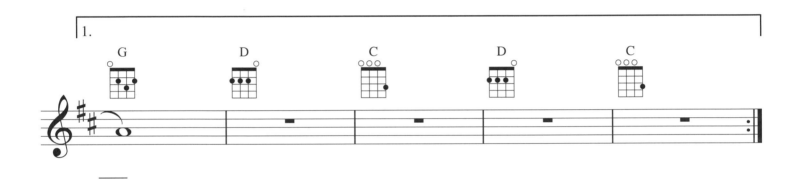

1.

_____

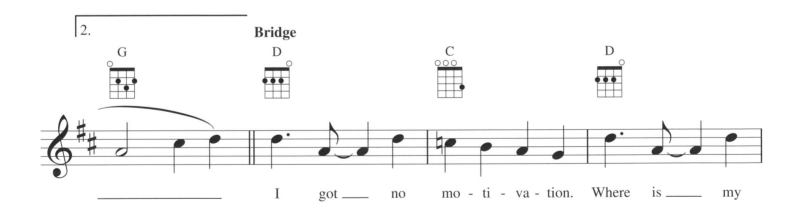

2.   **Bridge**

_____ I got _____ no mo - ti - va - tion. Where is _____ my

mo - ti - va - tion? No time _____ for a mo - ti - va - tion. Smok - ing _____ my

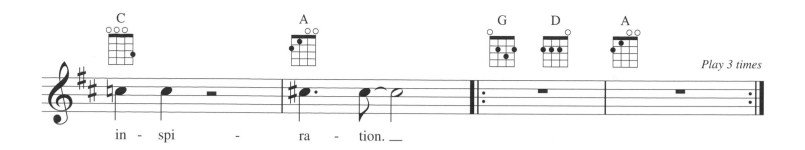

in - spi - ra - tion. __

Play 3 times

D.S. al Coda

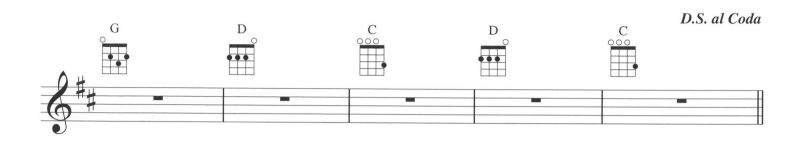

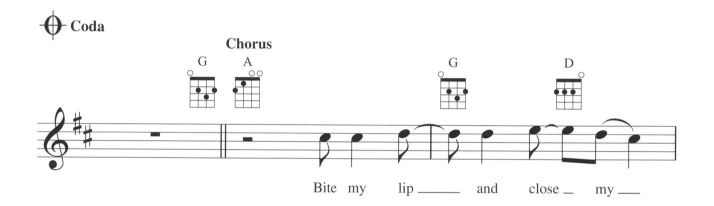

⊕ **Coda**

Chorus

Bite my lip ____ and close ___ my ___

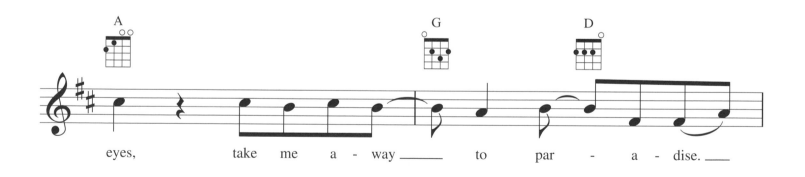

eyes, take me a - way ____ to par - a - dise. __

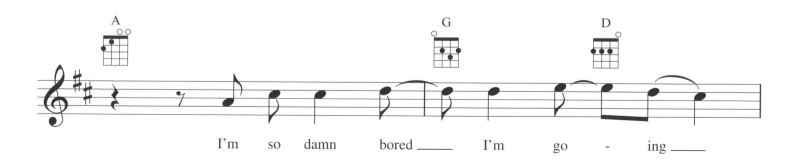

I'm so damn bored ____ I'm go - ing ____

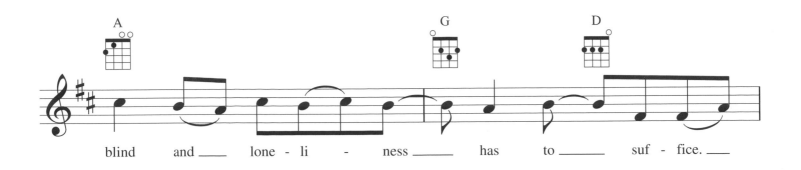

blind and ___ lone - li - ness ___ has to ___ suf - fice. ___

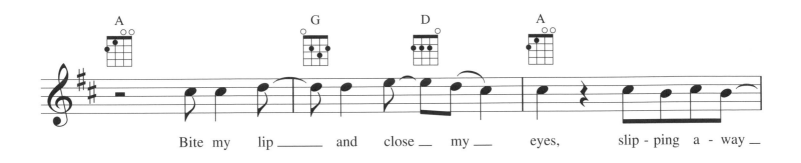

Bite my lip ___ and close ___ my ___ eyes, slip - ping a - way ___

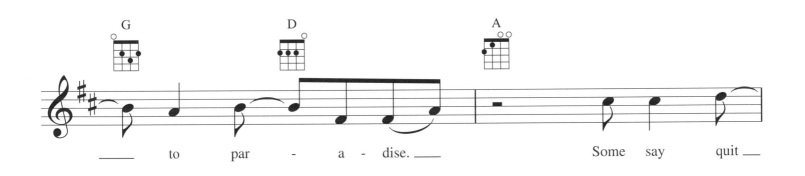

___ to par - a - dise. ___ Some say quit ___

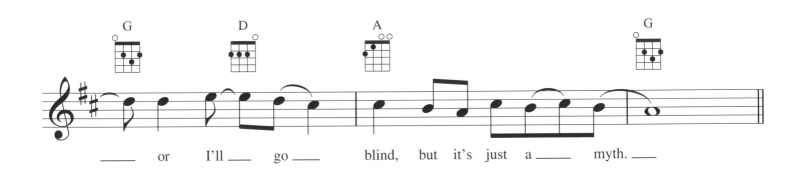

___ or I'll ___ go ___ blind, but it's just a ___ myth. ___

Outro

Repeat and fade

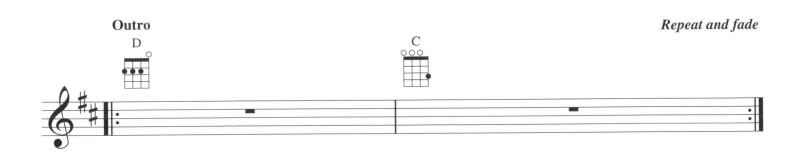

24

21 Guns

Words and Music by David Bowie, John Phillips, Billie Joe and Green Day

First note

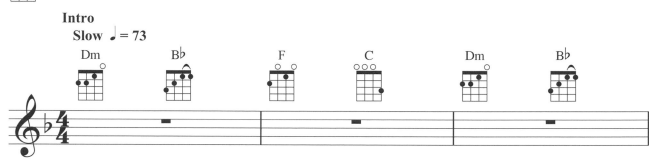

Intro
Slow ♩ = 73

Verse
Moderately slow ♩ = 79

1. Do you know what's worth fight - ing for, ____
2. When you're at the ____ end of the road, ___

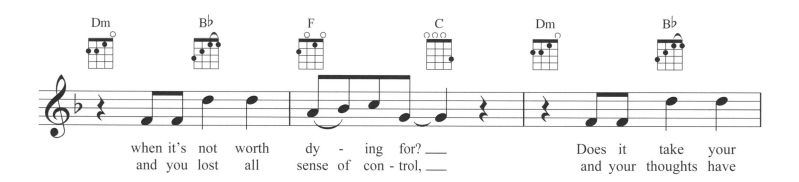

when it's not worth dy - ing for? __ Does it take your
and you lost all sense of con - trol, ___ and your thoughts have

breath __ a - way ___ and you feel _____ your - self suf - fo - cat -
tak - en their toll, ___ when your mind ____ breaks the spir - it of your

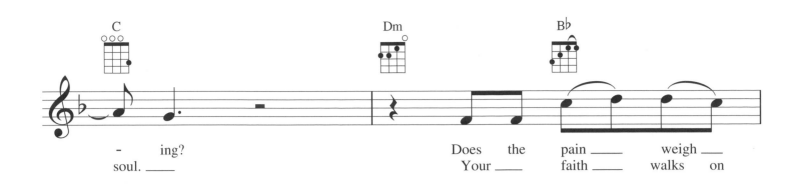

- ing?   Does the   pain ___ weigh ___
soul. ___   Your ___   faith ___   walks on

out ___ the pride? ___   And you look for a   place _ to hide? ___
bro - ken glass, ___   and the hang - o - ver   does - n't pass. ___

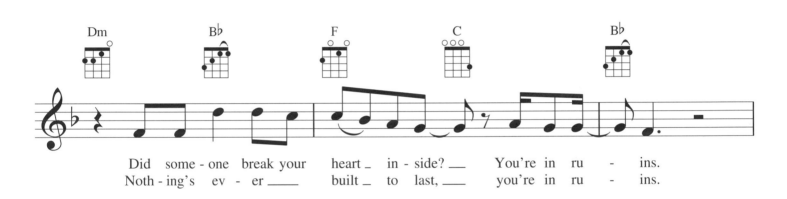

Did some - one break your   heart _ in - side? ___   You're in ru - ins.
Noth - ing's ev - er ___   built _ to last, ___   you're in ru - ins.

𝄋 **Chorus**

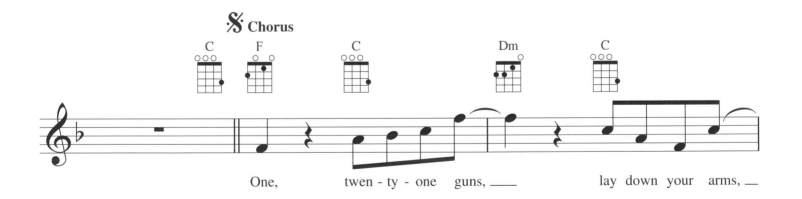

One,   twen - ty - one guns, ___   lay down your arms, ___

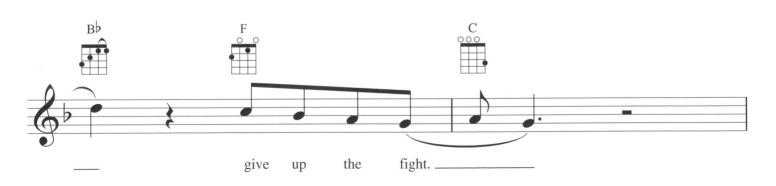

___   give up the   fight. ___

One, twen-ty-one guns, ___ throw up your arms ___ in-to the sky, ___

___ you and I ___

1.

2.

Bridge

Did you try to ___

live on your own, ___ when you burned down the house and home? ___

Did you stand too ___ close to the fi-re? Like a li-

- ar look-ing for for-give-ness from a stone. ___

Interlude

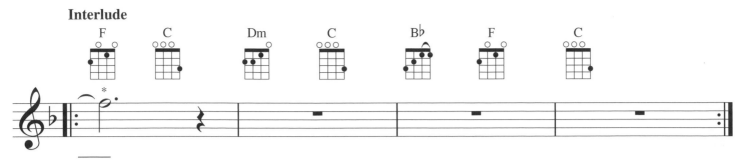

*Sung 1st time only.

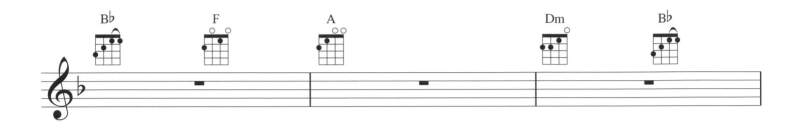

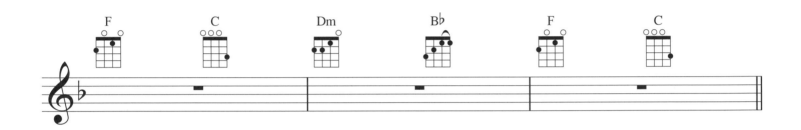

Verse

3. When it's time to ___ live and let die ___ and you can't get an -

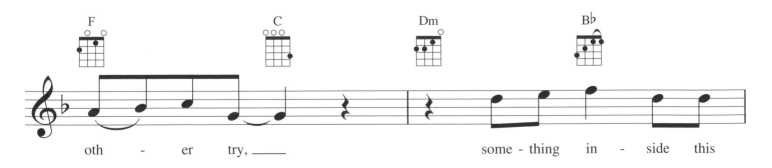

oth - er try, ___ some - thing in - side this

28

heart __ has died, __ you're in ru - ins.

Coda

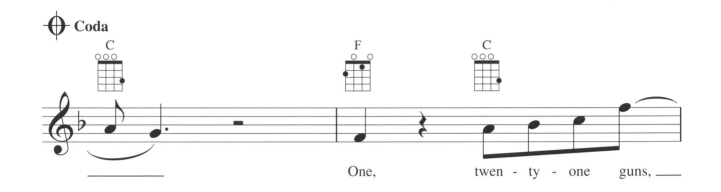

_____ One, twen - ty - one guns, ____

____ lay down your arms, __ give up the fight. _____

One, twen - ty - one guns, _____ throw up your arms ___ in - to the sky, __

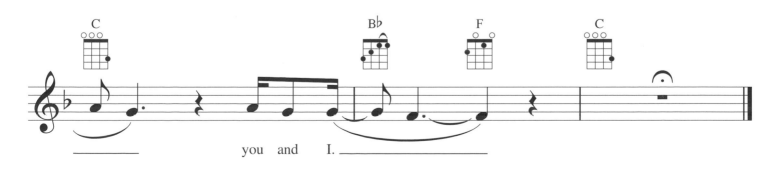

_____ you and I. _____

When I Come Around

Words by Billie Joe
Music by Green Day

TRACK 15

First note

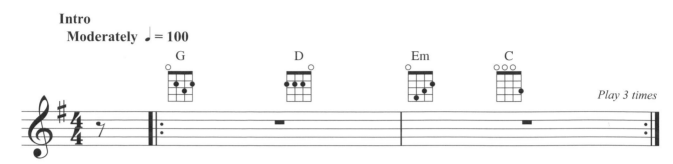

Intro
Moderately ♩ = 100

Play 3 times

Verse

1. Well, I heard you cry - in' loud ____
2. Well, I heard it all be - fore, ____

all the way _____ a - cross town. ____   You've been search -
so don't knock down my door. ____   I'm a lo -

- ing for that some - one, and it's me ____ out on the prowl, ____ as
- ser and a us - er so I don't ____ need no ac - cus - er to

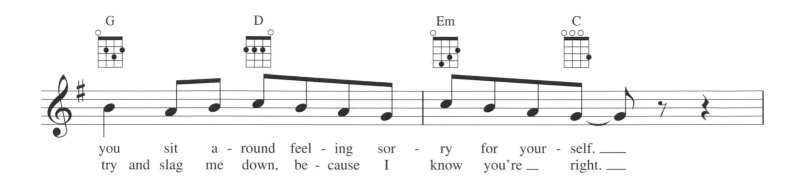

you sit a - round feel - ing sor - ry for your - self. ___
try and slag me down, be - cause I know you're ___ right. ___

Well, don't get lone - ly now, ____
So go do what you ___ like, ____

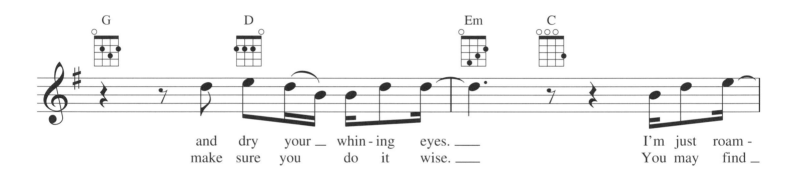

and dry your ___ whin - ing eyes. ___   I'm just roam -
make sure you do it wise. ___   You may find _

- ing for the mo - ment, sleaz - ing my _____ back - yard, so don't ___ get so ___
___ out that your self - doubt means no - thing was ev - er there. _____ You

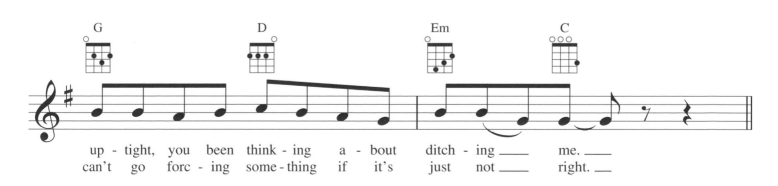

up - tight, you been think - ing a - bout ditch - ing _____ me. ___
can't go forc - ing some - thing if it's just not _____ right. ___

Chorus

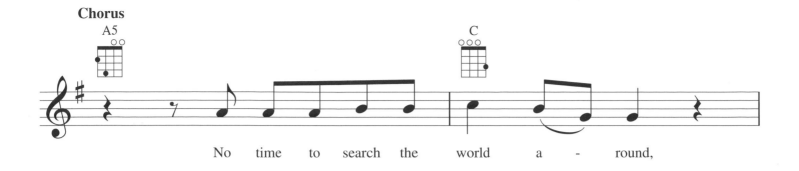

No time to search the world a - round,

'cause you know ___ where ___ I'll be found when I come a - round. ___

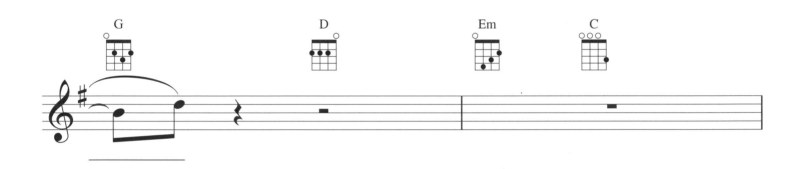

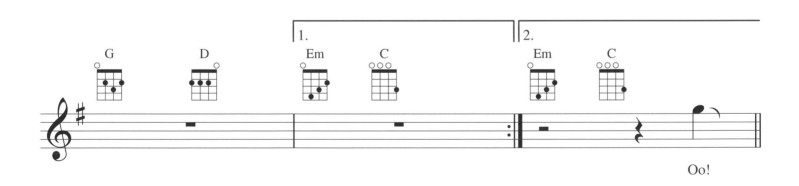

Oo!

Guitar Solo

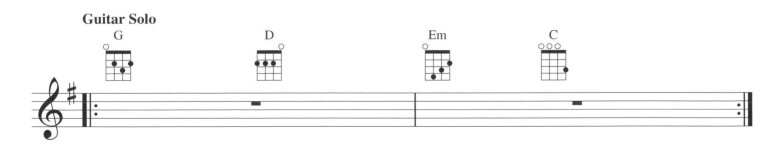

Chorus

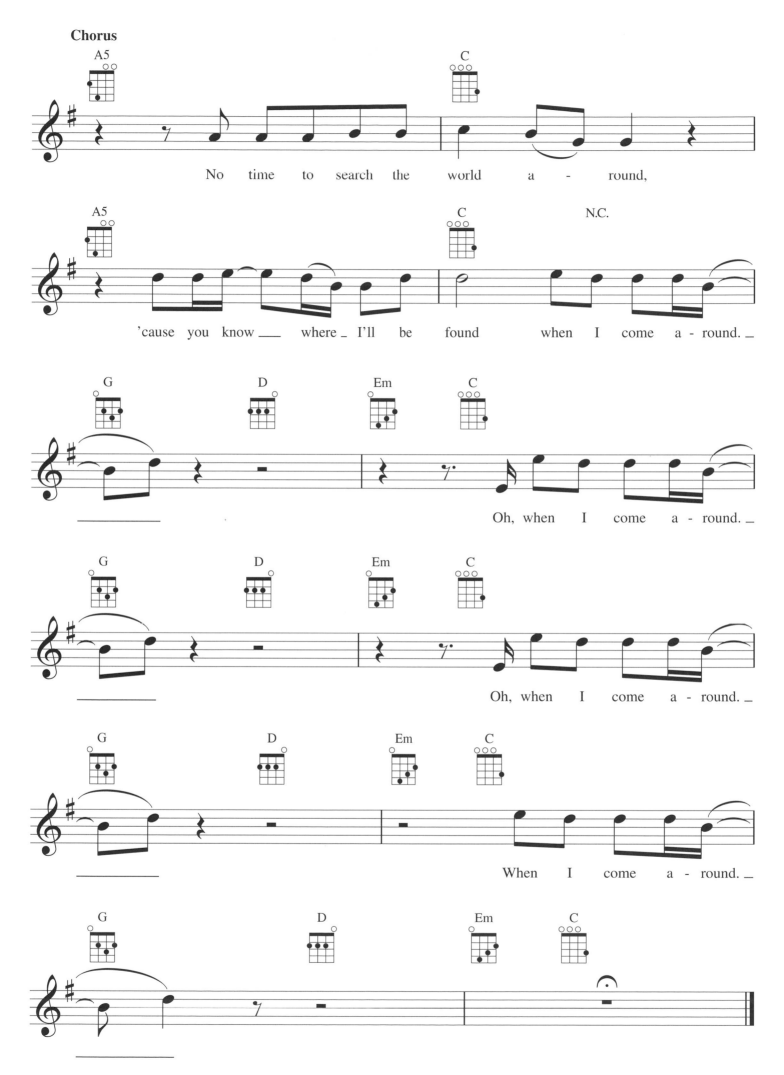

No time to search the world a - round,

'cause you know ___ where _ I'll be found when I come a - round. _

Oh, when I come a - round. _

Oh, when I come a - round. _

When I come a - round. _

Wake Me Up When September Ends

Words by Billie Joe
Music by Green Day

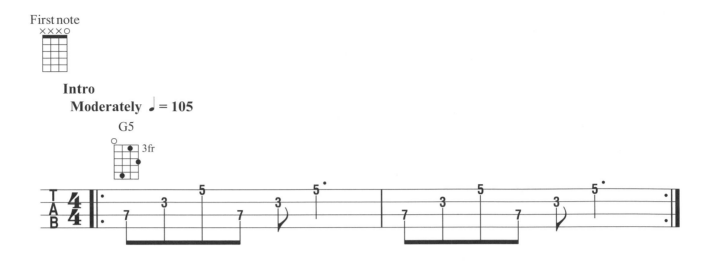

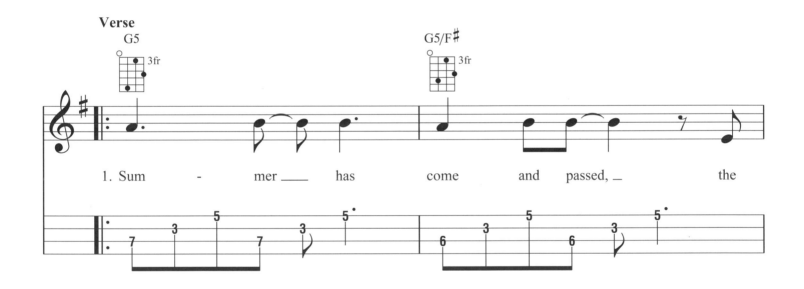

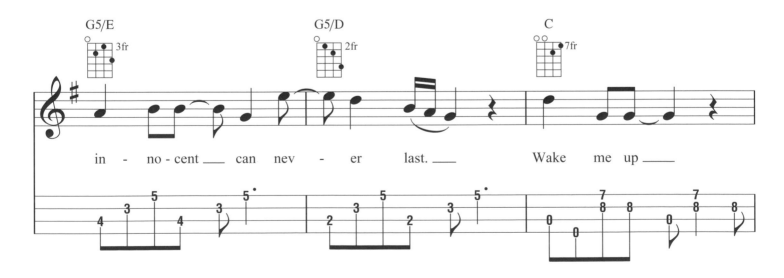

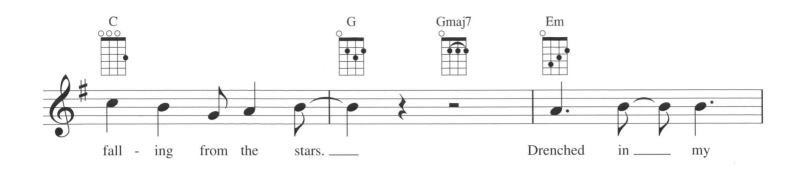

fall - ing from the stars. _____ Drenched in _____ my

pain a - gain, _____ be - com - ing who we _____ are. _____

Verse

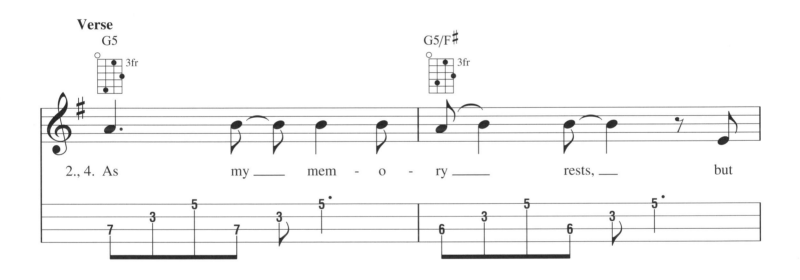

2., 4. As my _____ mem - o - ry _____ rests, _____ but

To Coda ✛

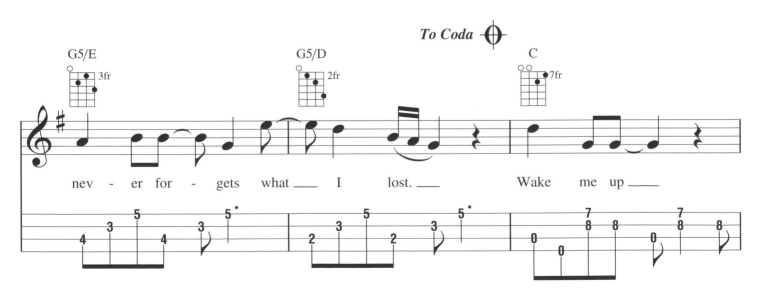

nev - er for - gets what _____ I lost. _____ Wake me up _____

when Sep - tem - ber ends. _____

Interlude

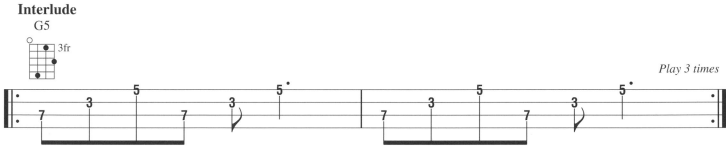

Play 3 times

Verse

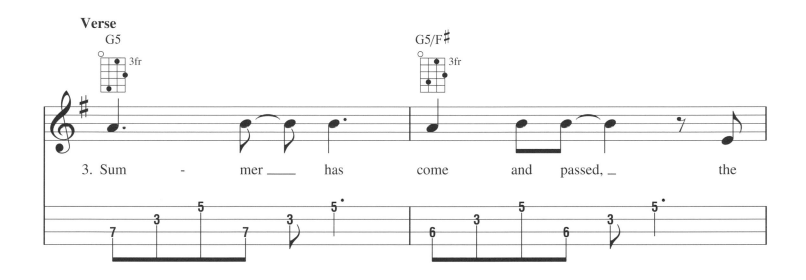

3. Sum - mer _____ has come and passed, _ the

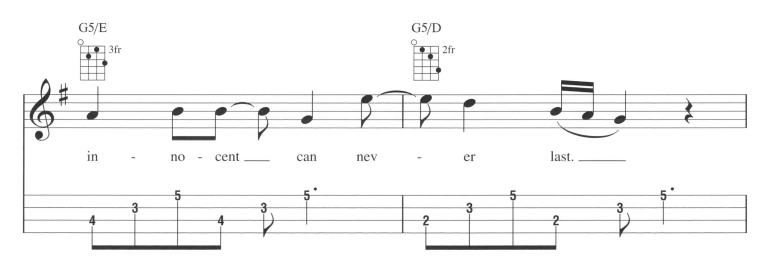

in - no - cent _____ can nev - er last. _____

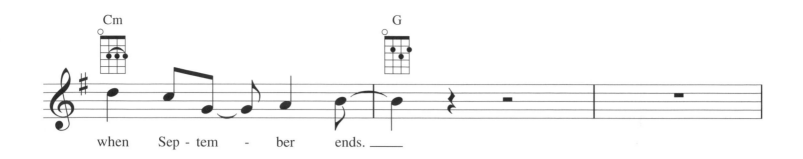

when Sep - tem - ber ends. ____

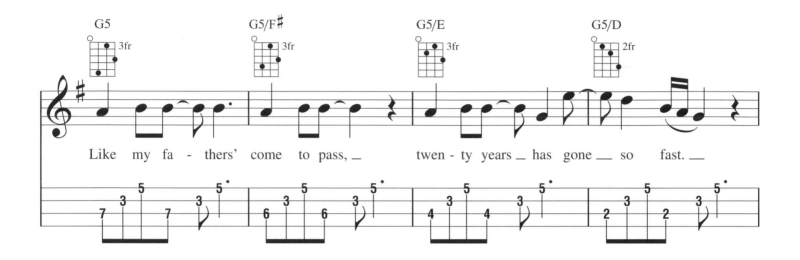

Like my fa - thers' come to pass, __ twen - ty years __ has gone __ so fast. __

Wake me up ____ when Sep - tem - ber ends. __

Wake me up ____ when Sep - tem - ber ends. __

Wake me up ____ when Sep - tem - ber ends. ____